More Time for You Now

Self-help Books

Susan Kersley

Published by Susan Kersley, 2024.

MORE TIME FOR YOU NOW

First edition. August 12, 2024.

ISBN: 979-8201188597

Written by Susan Kersley.

Table of Contents

Table of Contents

1.Introduction

In this book, you can read about the importance of time management, find out about techniques for effective time management, and discover practical ways to develop this essential skill.

When you read this book, you will discover ways to manage your time and your life. Some of these strategies will be familiar to you already. I hope that reading them again will motivate you to try them once more.

Time management, or life management, is one of those ill-defined concepts that seems easy in theory but turns out to be more challenging in practice.

However, the tips I offer you here, and in my other books, have been useful in enabling me to get stuff done and understand better why I cannot achieve other things!

There may be some you haven't discovered before. Please put them into practice, because without action on your part your time management won't improve. However, just a few of these will noticeably improve the way you achieve and get things done.

Like you, I sometimes get things done efficiently and quickly. Other times, I procrastinate and don't make progress.

If you have too much to do and not enough time, this book is for you. You've read, many times, what to do and been to workshops and lectures to give you the way to do just that - to manage your time and your life more effectively. Yet, you haven't been able to put those ideas into practice.

It's time to try again!

2. Don't wait for time to pass you by.

It can be easy to fall into the trap of waiting for the right moment to act. However, time waits for no one. It is constantly moving forward, and, with each passing minute, opportunities come and go.

Don't wait for the perfect occasion that may never come. There are benefits from acting and making the most of the present.

So, do not hesitate, or wait for the stars to align before making a move. It's essential to take control of your time and not let it slip away.

Are you one of those people who resists making changes because you have mastered the skill of procrastination?

Reasons used to delay taking the action you say you want to make, are:

- It's not the right time to make changes.
- I'm not in the right place to do that.
- I haven't got my mind around it yet, so won't do it.
- I don't know how to start.
- Other people won't like it if I change things.
- I'm not that sort of person to do things differently.

Are these your excuses for not doing something? You sound convincing when you tell others what you'd really like to do but stay stuck in your rut. Change these statements from negative to positive. Your perception of what is possible will change.

Affirmations are part of your roadmap for success.

Go through each excuse and turn it around so it becomes the reason to succeed.

Here are examples of statements to use for achievement:

- It's the right time to overcome any obstacles.
- I'm in the right place to solve the problems.
- I've got my mind around it to accomplish what I want.
- I know what to do to achieve.
- My life and how I live matters to me.
- I am the person who succeeds.

This is your time to do things. Instead of waiting, clarify your goals and plan your course of action. Whoever you are, there are ways you can achieve what you want.

You can engage your project with a positive mindset so that you overcome obstacles to move forward with your goals.

Decide what you want and the steps you must take to achieve it. Become aware of your own wish to succeed. Make your changes into a win-win situation for those affected.

3. Learning to manage your time.

Effective time management is a crucial skill for success in both your personal and professional life. Learning to manage your time efficiently can lead to increased productivity, reduced stress, and a better work-life balance.

By prioritising tasks, setting goals, and using effective time management, you can improve your daily routines and achieve your objectives.

Whether you are a student, a professional, or someone looking to make the most of your time, mastering the art of time management will bring about positive changes in your life.

Time management isn't always easy. Perhaps this is because you are used to working long hours, saying 'yes' to whatever others ask of you, and forgetting the importance of looking after yourself and your own self-care needs.

If you constantly feel stressed and overwhelmed with how much you attempt to fit into your day, then improving your time management skills will help.

Just like other aspects of life, managing your time is something you have to learn. It involves a change in your behaviour, and you may find initially that you slip back into your previous habits.

To absorb and put into practice any new skill, practise the basics. Then do what you've learned not just once or twice but repeat your new behaviour at least twenty-one times. Doing this means that the habit changes from something you must think about to something that you will do automatically.

For example, decide that you would have more time if you said 'no' more often when people ask you to do them a favour.

At first you may feel guilty about this. Your excuse seems a poor reason to refuse, especially when they say no-one else can help. You've got to be firm and not waver, just keep saying 'no, I can't do it' or 'no, I've got something else to do,' until they get the message!

You must learn more efficient ways to complete tasks, so you aren't wasting time. Gain enough confidence to say 'no' to others but also 'no' to the task itself, if it has lost its purpose. Perhaps no-one understands why it needs to be done at all.

When your stress levels rise, you wonder what the most important thing you could do to feel calmer. Managing your time successfully is vital.

Time management is about organising your life more effectively. When you do, you become much clearer about what you're trying to achieve and can work out useful ways to do this. You also find, when you plan your day, that you get more things done and, by achieving goals quickly, you feel more in control and less stressed.

4. Best way to manage time?

From meeting deadlines at work to fulfilling personal commitments, effective time management can help you achieve your goals and maintain a healthy work-life balance.

Explore the best ways to manage your time effectively. There are strategies and techniques that can help you achieve more and reduce stress.

If you manage your time, you are organising your life more effectively. The two are intertwined, so getting to grips with one affects the other.

Stephen Covey in his book *'The seven habits of highly effective people'* recommends that classifying your daily activities as follows.

. Here are some ways to start:

1. Decide whether something is urgent and/or important or neither.
2. Concentrate on tasks which are important but not urgent. Plan important tasks before they become urgent.
3. Deal quickly with what is urgent and important.
4. Deal with those that are urgent though not important.
5. Eliminate tasks which are neither urgent nor important.

Decide if what you want to do is:

- urgent and important
- urgent and not important
- not urgent and important
- not urgent and not important.

When you think about your activities in relation to these quadrants, become aware of how you spend your time and how you need to change what you do.

Many people spend a vast amount of time doing things that are **urgent but not important**. An example of these activities would be answering the phone, talking to people who interrupt your flow of work, and responding to someone knocking at your door.

If something is urgent, then you must attend to it. For example, if you are a doctor and somebody collapses, then you must deal with it immediately. However, aim to do most of your tasks in the quadrant that is for things that are **important and not urgent**. When you know that a certain piece of work has to be done with a deadline, divide the work over the time available rather than trying to do it all the day before. The more you plan what you're going to do means that you gradually get your tasks completed and are less stressed.

Think about the things you do which are **not urgent and not important** and eliminate as many of these as possible. Of course, these may include activities you need for your rest and relaxation, or they may purely be time wasters such as watching too much television.

Whether it's juggling work deadlines, household chores, social commitments, or personal projects, the pressure can be all-consuming. This feeling of having too much to do, can lead to stress, burnout, and a sense of never being able to catch up, overwhelmed by your tasks and the impact it can have on your mental and physical well-being.

5.Decide what to achieve each day.

If you say to yourself: 'the day isn't long enough to do all that...' then **better time management** is the answer. Something must change. You could start with your attitude to daily tasks.

Before you go to bed, get into the habit of thinking about what you would like to do tomorrow. Note on paper, computer, or smart phone, a list of tasks. As you do each cross them off your list.

If what you plan involves equipment or special clothing or a certain file, then get those ready beforehand.

Make a realistic plan for the day and know when you will engage with each task, then you are more likely to get those things done. The important thing is that your plan includes the specific job or part of a job that you want to complete rather than a vague 'get on with such-and-such' statement.

Get going so that routine tasks are out of the way quickly so you can spend as much time as possible doing what you love to do. Start early, get the things you don't like done, then move onto other tasks until you complete what you plan to do.

Use efficient ways to complete the tasks.

There are ways to work more quickly and getting on with the job. This might include improving your basic skills so you can do things confidently or delegating to others either on an exchange basis or for payment.

Match similar tasks.

Devise strategies to do similar tasks consecutively to save time. Being efficient also means not wasting time by noticing how you spend your day and how much of it you are engaged in productive things and how much fritters away.

What doesn't have to be done?

Habits become automatic relatively quickly, after about twenty-one repetitions. Think about your daily routine and question if you need to be doing things that have become habits. You are likely to find some that no longer have any reason, and these are things to dump.

If you are frustrated because you want to do more, you must become more time-aware and recognise how you spend your day. Do this by logging what you do for a couple of days. Note every fifteen minutes, for example. Then it will be easier to identify where to make changes. You will discover what you could do differently.

There may be **more efficient ways** to organise your work. It's easy to get into a routine of doing something a particular way. Ask a friend or colleague for their opinion about whether there might be a quicker way to do your jobs.

You can devise a **system to automate** part or all of what you do. Let go of your need to do everything, or the belief that only you can do a good job. Delegate more to others. Recognise that some of what you cram into your day could be done by someone else. Train them in the skills needed and check until you are sure they are doing the job the way you want it done.

Stop doing some things. Re-assess your regular habits to check whether they remain useful.

6. Plan your day the evening before.

Planning your day ahead can have a profound impact on your overall well-being. By taking a few moments each evening to plan what to do the next day, you can set yourself up for success.

There are many ways to get yourself and your life more organised. If you are wasting time and opportunities regularly, you need to find and follow a way to use your day more efficiently and effectively.

Planning your day the previous evening is the way to get more order into your life. Whether you like this method depends on you. If you don't enjoy working and living following a pre-planned timetable, which may bring back memories of being at school or working with tight demands on your time, you may prefer to greet each day anew with not much idea at the start of it where it and your spirit will lead you.

However, it can be a great motivator if you spend a few moments each evening thinking about, and then deciding, about what you want to get done during the following day. It's important, as always, to be specific and realistic about this.

The other important thing to do, whatever you decide, is to write it down. The mere act of writing something consolidates it in your mind and you will be much more likely to achieve your intentions.

There is also a balance to be struck between aiming too high and aiming too low when deciding what you want to get done. If you want to achieve more than you are realistically capable, then you may feel as though you have failed in your chosen task or you may find that you can do far more than you initially hoped, which is a great morale booster and self-esteem raiser.

Going for something that is too easy means you will have the satisfaction of achieving quickly and you may even become bored with the subject. On the positive side you'll get more done, more quickly and could feel a great satisfaction at your rapid achievements.

Resolve to give this method a try, each evening, for the next three weeks. Write what you want to get done and monitor what comes into your life during that time. If you find this useful for becoming more organised, then continue with it.

7. Is everything related to work?

Do you feel as though your life revolves around work. From the moment you wake up to the minute you go to bed, you are bombarded with emails, meetings, deadlines, and the constant pressure to always be "on." But is everything in your day truly related to work? Do you allow your job to consume every aspect of your life or is there more to your daily routine than work?

Explore the impact that work has on your daily life and investigate whether everything you do is truly work-related. Look at the blurred lines between work and personal time, the importance of setting boundaries, and the potential consequences of letting work take over your life. By examining the role that work plays in your daily routine, you will gain a better understanding of how to achieve a healthy work-life balance.

Does every waking hour have you thinking and worrying about what you did, what you said, or how you are going to deal with a situation in relation to your work?

Have you forgotten what leisure time is and wish for time for yourself to catch up with friends and things at home that need doing? If thoughts of time for relaxing or pursuing hobbies seem impossible, then do things differently.

Does life have to be like that forever? You may believe there is no option except to continue your life in the same way but ignore the consequences for your health and well-being.

As you become more stressed, you find you don't sleep well, you eat too much and drink too much alcohol.

You use caffeine to keep alert to get all the jobs completed within a time frame.

But it doesn't have to be like that. Is life worth living if you have no time for anything except work? Turn over a new leaf and care for yourself more. This means being clear about how you spend your time and when to stop working and in order to do other things.

At a certain point of the day, resolve to put your papers away, close your computer and leave your desk. Then pick up your swimming things, your sports equipment, your musical instrument, your novel or whatever you need for your leisure. Anything that involves exercise or creativity is ideal to re-charge your personal batteries and take your mind and body away from the stress of work.

At first you may feel guilty when you do non-work-related activities there is a surprising effect: you return with renewed energy and enthusiasm and can cope much better with the work. Your brain is clearer; you find solutions to problems quickly and complete tasks effectively. Doing something outside of work increases your enjoyment of life and improves your health and well-being enormously.

Relax. Try working hard for an hour or two and then take a break. Get some fresh air and take some exercise. When you do this, you return refreshed because your brain recharges and your energy increases.

When you take regular breaks, you are more motivated to continue and get the work and studying completed.

8.What has most effect on your time?

Time is one of the most valuable resources in your life, yet it is something of which you have a finite amount. Every day, you face decisions and distractions that either help you make the most of your time or not.

There are a multitude of factors that influence how you choose to spend your time.

If you feel rushed off your feet, always under pressure to get things done in a short time, the most important thing is to be clear about what you will or won't do for yourself and for others. Do not be afraid to say 'no' loudly and clearly when you realise what you do isn't working for your energy levels.

For example, someone suggests you watch a programme on television or read a particular book, or see a new film, because they say it is incredibly interesting and you will enjoy it. However, when you watch or read it because someone said you should do so, this eats into your time. Before you know it, you no longer have any time left to do what you'd planned to do that day. Maybe you would have preferred to do some gardening, go for a walk or read a book of your own choice.

Even though you promise your friend you would keep watching or reading in order to discuss it later together, you resent using the time you wanted to use for some other activity, so any discussion will not be enjoyable.

Be clear about what you really want to do and say 'no' clearly and assertively. Tell your friend that you have other things to do which are more important now for you.

When you say 'no' to things that you do as a favour for someone else, a weight lifts from your mind and you feel renewed energy and enthusiasm for other things. You experience a big bonus of having more time to do what you want.

Start today and only say 'yes' to something you want to do and practise saying 'no' more often.

Effective time management is an important skill that can significantly impact all aspects of your life. From meeting deadlines at work to making time for self-care, how you manage your time can influence your success and wellbeing. By understanding the factors with the most effect on your time management you can learn how to better select what to do first and have a better work-life balance. The key elements that can help you make the most of your time are:

Define precisely what you could achieve in a specified amount of time. 'An extra hour each day, means I would keep my accounts up to date,' or 'With an extra day each month I would visit all the Art exhibitions in my area.'

What benefits would you experience as a result?

- Improved self-confidence.
- Better health and wellbeing.
- Positive approach to work.

Plan to include all the steps to reach your goal. A timetable for what to do each day and complete by the end of the month. When you set goals, you are more likely to achieve them. When you know what you hope to get done during each day, you gradually move towards completing your goal.

Sometimes life takes over, and you may not achieve what you planned. Flexibility gives you the chance to catch up on days when you are doing things quickly.

Take action to follow through with your plans. You already know what you want and how to achieve. You remain stuck because you don't act.

What's stopping you, what obstacles are in your way? It is your beliefs, your thoughts, about what might happen.

9. Important ways to have more time.

It can often feel like there simply aren't enough hours in the day. Finding ways to create more time for the things that truly matter can seem like a vague goal, but with the right plans, it is indeed possible to create space for what brings you happiness and make the most of every precious moment in your day.

There are important ways you can have more time and live a more balanced, fulfilling life. By applying these, you can be more productive, and proactive in how you manage your time, leading to a greater sense of control and satisfaction in your daily life.

To manage your day, be clear about what you want to get done. Decide what you hope to achieve by the end of the week, by the end of the month, and by the end of the year. Until you know what you want to achieve, how will you know when you've got there?

Get organised.

If your life and possessions are chaotic and you feel as though you never have enough time to do what you want to do, then spend a designated amount of time getting more organised.

Make sure your workspace is clear except for whatever you need in order to get on with the job you have set yourself.

Put things away and keep similar things together so that it's easy to find them again. Throw away papers and other things that you no longer need.

Become better at 'letting things go'. When your surrounding space becomes more organised, so does your thinking and you will do much more in a short time and do some things that, now, you don't have time for.

Keep focussed.

If you are distracted easily, it's important to train yourself to divide your tasks into small steps so that you can finish one step at a time and gradually move forward to achieving all your goals.

Vary what you do.

A great way to keep motivated is to vary what you do during the day. You may find, for example, that changing the type of task you do every hour is an effective way to get several things done during the day. This works best if you change from a desk-based activity to doing something that involves more physical movement.

Acknowledge what you get done.

Some people get frustrated when they feel they are not achieving very much. However, if you devise a way to note when you finish each step of your project, then you will be more aware of how you are progressing.

Get things done.

Sort out what must be done by making lists or using mind-mapping. You can do this manually using paper and pen or on the computer with mind-mapping software. The advantage of mind-mapping is that it represents what you are planning to do in a non-linear way and it's easier to find connections between your different tasks.

Know what you want to achieve during the day.

When you are more organised, you will have increased clarity about what needs to be done each day. You'll find that having a specific goal to work towards enables you to work more efficiently and quickly and so makes it more likely that some time will become available.

Do as much as you can within a set period.

Decide to work on a project and do as much as possible within, for example, half an hour. It is a common experience that you can do much more than you thought you could. If you know you have the entire day to get something done, you work more slowly and achieve very much less.

Prepare tasks the day before.

It is always useful to think about what you need to do before what you plan. Sometimes you need to find references, look something up on the Internet, make a phone call, or talk to somebody about the job you are about to undertake. These are the preliminary tasks that need to be done before you can do the main bulk of the work.

Be clear about what to do later.

When you follow the suggestions, you will become motivated to work quickly, get things done efficiently and as a result will find more time to do other things apart from the project you're involved in. You will therefore have the opportunity for more exercise and more creative activities or whatever you plan to do with the time you free up, by working in this way.

10. Writing a to-do list.

Creating and maintaining a to-do list is a powerful way to manage your time and stay organised.

A well-structured to-do list can be a lifesaver. Whether you are a student trying to balance coursework and extracurricular activities, a professional running multiple projects at work, or simply someone looking to stay on top of your daily tasks, learning how to write an effective to-do list is a skill that can benefit you.

It is a well-known saying that people who write what they want to achieve are many more times likely to succeed.

When you write what you would like to do each day, this will enable you to keep concentrating on what you plan to do.

Writing a to-do list will help to stop you from flitting from one task to another and help to keep you focussed on what need to be done. It is very motivating to tick off the jobs as you do them and see the list getting smaller.

However, there is still the temptation to neglect some things that you should have done because either you don't put them on the list or ignore them even though on it. If you have a to-do list, you need to discover the reasons you procrastinate and why you ignore some of it.

Do you put off doing some things because you don't know how to do it, or because doing that task is against your personal values, or you don't believe it needs to be done. Ask yourself why. Sometimes it's better to get those things you really don't want to do over first thing in the day, so you have the rest of the day to do those enjoyable things.

There are various practical ways to write a to-do list. Your to-do list can be a vertical list or as a mind-map. A list places one task under another with no sign of the importance or urgency of the task. There is the temptation to start at the top and work through the list from top to bottom.

A mind map is a representation of the way your mind works and allows you to make connections between the different tasks. To draw a mind map, start with your paper as landscape and write a word such as ' to do' in the centre of the page with a line drawn around it. Then take lines radiating out from it with drawings or more words of what must be done. Each subject will suggest more words and tasks related to it. You will end up with a scatter diagram across the page and it's easy to see which things connect. You can use coloured pens to join these and realise what tasks can go together. A mind mapped to-do list is the way to go for more efficiency.

By creating a comprehensive and organised list of tasks, you can be clear on what is important, concentrate on what needs to be accomplished, and ultimately free up more time for the things that truly matter to you.

One way to organise your time more effectively is by writing your to-do list.

Notice the word: 'write.' Some people believe so long as you keep what needs to be done in your head you can easily get everything done.

But that doesn't always work, does it? You reach the end of the day and suddenly remember who to contact or what task to do.

Train yourself to follow a new habit. Write your to-do list each day: doing this enables you to keep focused on what you plan to do instead of flitting from one thought to another and one task to another and then finding that you have neglected some things that you should have done.

There will always be more tasks to add to the end of your list. Make sure you re-write your list every day or two. When you look back over the number of things you have crossed off because you've done them or decided they don't need to be done, you will be very pleased with yourself and what you've achieved.

Look at what you've written and notice if you've been quite specific about what you will do. Next notice if two or more tasks relate to each other so you can decide the right order to approach doing them. Most of all, try the writing a list technique and notice how many more things you get done.

11. What's most important?

Time management is an important skill that everyone must master to juggle the demands of work, personal life, and leisure activities. This can make the difference in achieving your goals and maintaining a healthy work-life balance.

There are numerous strategies and techniques that can be used to improve time management, one important aspect stands out as the most important - self-awareness.

Understanding your personal strengths and weaknesses, knowing your most efficient times, and identifying your main concerns are essential components of effective time management. By being aware of your own habits and tendencies, you can develop a time management plan that supports your goals.

The significance of self-awareness in time management and practical tips and plans to help you with the best use of time. From setting realistic goals to overcoming procrastination, there are key principles that help you make the most of your day and achieve greater efficiency and satisfaction in all areas of your life.

By self-awareness and taking active steps to manage your time wisely, you can improve your efficiency, reduce stress, and ultimately, lead a more fulfilling and balanced life.

If important tasks don't get done, complete those things first before the unimportant jobs.

If you spend the start of each working session doing unimportant and non-urgent tasks such as browsing the internet, then one thing follows another, you become less focussed and almost forget the task you had been engaged in before you got onto the Internet.

It's a useful exercise to decide the most important thing you must do tomorrow. Leave your working place with the folders ready on your desk so when you start work the next day you can get straight into the job without further delay.

Clarity means doing jobs when you are fresh, and before you get bogged down in less important tasks.

Don't waste time on long telephone conversations or prolonged coffee breaks. When you have sorted out your priorities for the day, speak to a colleague or make a phone call to move that task to its conclusion. That's fine.

Plan to meet deadlines in good time. Start moving towards what you want. Doing something reluctantly makes the task take longer. Find someone else to do it.

Set yourself a time limit for doing tasks such as checking emails, rather than each time an email arrives in your inbox.

Don't stop what you are doing to answer the telephone. Deal with messages on the phone later.

Notice and act on what you discover.

Ask yourself how much of your routine tasks must be done at all.

12. Reduce stress.

The ability to effectively manage your time is vital. Time management is not just about planning activities and meetings; it is about making deliberate choices on how you spend your precious hours to get the most out of each day. Effective time management can significantly reduce stress levels and increase overall well-being.

Practising good time management can help you lead a more balanced and stress-free life. From deciding what is urgent, reducing distractions and practising self-care, you will discover ways to help you reduce the stress in your life.

If your stress levels are rising, feel calmer and more in control of what you are doing, by managing your time.

What is an important tool to help you manage your time and reduce your stress?

How can you overcome the challenges of having too much to do?

After thinking about your daily routine and dumping anything that doesn't have to be done, are you using your time doing something which you could delegate to someone else? Pay someone to help you, arrange an exchange of services or discover you don't enjoy doing something that someone else loves to do. Explain what you want and spend some time teaching another person what to do.

If you consider yourself an organised person and yet you procrastinate about getting things done, then you need to consider whether you have too much mental or physical clutter which make you delay completing tasks. You may not realise how this can affect your ability to get on and do what you want.

13. Delegate more.

Delegating tasks is a crucial skill to master. By sharing responsibilities, you not only lighten your workload, but also empowers others to develop new skills and take ownership of their work. However, many people struggle with letting go of control and may hesitate to delegate tasks out of fear that they will not be completed to their standards.

An important principle for managing your time and your life more effectively is to stop doing unnecessary tasks and then getting into the habit of delegating tasks which must be done, though not necessarily by you.

Whether you or someone else does these tasks it should go without saying that they should be done effectively. By delegating and discussing the task with someone, you may find that you learn more efficient ways to achieve the same result more quickly.

This might be a challenge for you if you are someone who believes you can do it more quickly and more efficiently than anyone else. For you, the thought of asking someone while expecting that they will take longer and do it less well than you, are huge obstacles, but overcome this mindset you must, for the sake of better work-life balance, less stress and more time available.

The reality is this: if you don't have enough time, if you feel overwhelmed and stressed because you have too much to do, then delegation must be the answer. It is vital to take some time to consider how to do this and who would be the person to whom you could delegate.

However, put some effort into the process initially to make sure it works well and is for everyone's benefit. Delegation works best when it becomes part of a 'win-win' situation so that not only you have more time for other things but also the person you delegate to also gains in terms of experience, pay or enjoyment.

Explain clearly to the person to whom you want to delegate, exactly what you want done and by when. Show them the procedures and make sure they also have the instructions in writing. Initially observe them following the process so you can be sure they understand what you require.

Explain and go over any parts that they haven't understood. Check until you are sure they know what you want. This process may take anything from a few hours to a few days. However, once it's done, you can be confident that your delegation will be successful.

Delegating more, letting go of some tasks completely and becoming much more efficient leads to:

◈ Being on time because you get your work done more quickly and effectively.

◈ Recognising the importance of self-care because there is more to life than work.

◈ Increasing the amount you exercise to look after your body.

◈ Rediscovering long forgotten hobbies, to nourish your mind and spirit.

◈ Becoming free from the tyranny of overwork, to enjoy the rest of life.

◈ Reducing your stress levels to be more relaxed.

◈ Having a more balanced life and know there is more to life than work.

You can't do everything so delegate to somebody else. Maybe this means paying someone to do a few of your routine tasks, such as housework or gardening.

It's easy to forget that you have committed to doing something for yourself unless you make a definite commitment to do so and that means putting it in your diary or on the calendar and treat it as important as any other appointment you may have there.

It's easy to dismiss your own needs if someone asks you to do something but if you treat your own needs as equally, if not more important than other people's requests, then you will develop the confidence to keep your own arrangements.

As you increase your ability to spend time on yourself, you find that there is a positive outcome in relation to your energy in doing things for others. You will set new boundaries in what you do for them and feel a great sense of satisfaction in what you can achieve for your own health and well-being.

When this happens, you can assess what you are doing with the rest of your day and how you could do that much more efficiently.

14. Mental clutter.

If your subconscious, or conscious, mind fills with 'mental clutter' then this slows you down so everything you do takes longer to complete. Get rid of worry, anger, and resentment, and notice how much more quickly you complete what you do.

Mental clutter refers to the overwhelming thoughts, worries, responsibilities, or information that occupy your mind and delay your ability to focus, think clearly, or make decisions. You may feel mentally overwhelmed, stressed, or anxious due to a constant stream of thoughts running through your mind. Mental clutter can result from factors such as information overload, unprocessed emotions, unfinished tasks, or a lack of organisation. Managing mental clutter is essential for maintaining mental well-being.

It's easy to feel overwhelmed by the constant thoughts, worries, and to-dos that clutter your mind. This can have a significant impact on your mental well-being and overall quality of life. Understanding what mental clutter is and how it affects you is important in managing your mental health.

Mental clutter can have a significant impact on your overall well-being.

Here are some ways in which mental clutter can affect you:

- When your mind is cluttered with various thoughts and worries, it can be difficult to focus and concentrate on tasks. This can lead to decreased efficiency in completing work or daily responsibilities.
- Mental clutter can contribute to feelings of stress and anxiety as your mind feels overwhelmed by the many thoughts running through it. This can lead to increased stress and can also impact

your ability to relax and unwind.

- Having a cluttered mind can make it harder to make decisions, as it can be challenging to sort through different thoughts. This may lead to indecisiveness and feeling stuck in your decision-making process.

- Mental clutter can also affect your memory and ability to concentrate. With so much going on in your mind, it becomes harder to retain information and focus on tasks at hand.

- Mental clutter can contribute to emotional distress and mood swings. When your mind is cluttered, it can be difficult to process and regulate your emotions effectively, leading to feelings of frustration, sadness, or irritability.

- Mental clutter can affect your relationships with others. It may lead to communication difficulties, misunderstandings, and a general sense of being disconnected from those around you.

Overall, mental clutter can have a significant impact on your mental and emotional well-being, as well as your ability to function effectively in various parts of your life. It is important to find ways to declutter your mind and manage your thoughts to maintain a healthy and balanced state of mind.

By gaining a better understanding of mental clutter and learning how to address it effectively, you can develop a more calm, focussed, and balanced mental state.

Worrying about what might happen. If you fill your mind with all the negative possibilities these are likely to stop you making progress. When your mind is filled with questions like, 'suppose this doesn't work' or what if I fail?' then you are likely to be stuck.

Remembering old resentments. If you keep on recalling a time when you tried to do something like what you are trying to do now and remember how someone treated you badly or inconsiderately, so much so that the memory inhibits you making further progress. Instead remind yourself that both you and the other person have moved on, and you are now able to deal with any adverse reaction you may have at this time from them.

Self-depreciation. Your self-talk can stop you moving forward when you hear yourself doing yourself down when you say negative things about yourself and your ability to complete what you are aiming to do. Instead become more aware of this self-talk and practice re-phrasing your words into something more positive.

Working to out-dated rules. Get into the habit of questioning your motives or reasons for doing certain things. Your actions or non-actions may be a reaction to what you were told about your abilities when you were a child. Your parents or teachers may have told you that you were no good at something or would never succeed in doing another thing and these messages may have stayed with you adding to your mental clutter.

Not making your own decisions. When you want to achieve something for yourself you need to become more confident about deciding some things for yourself. If you are not achieving because of mental clutter, then you may have filled your mind with numerous opinions from others about what you should or shouldn't do. The more opinions you ask from others the more you can become informed about the situation and so be better qualified to make the best decision for yourself. However eventually make the choice, yourself, about what to do.

Here are some ways to get rid of mental clutter:

- Keep a journal or to-do list to write down your thoughts, tasks, and ideas. This can help clear your mind and allows you to focus on the present moment.
- Engage in activities that help you stay present and focused,

such as meditation, deep breathing, or yoga. This can help reduce stress and improve mental clarity.

- A cluttered environment can contribute to mental clutter. Take some time to declutter your home or workspace to create a more organised and peaceful environment.
- Make a list of tasks based on importance and urgency. Focus on completing one task at a time to avoid feeling overwhelmed.
- Identify distractions that may be contributing to your mental clutter, such as excessive screen time or multitasking. Set boundaries and create designated times for work and relaxation.
- Give yourself permission to take breaks and recharge when needed. Stepping away from your work or responsibilities can help clear your mind and improve focus.
- If you are struggling to manage your mental clutter, consider talking to a therapist or counsellor for support and guidance.

Remember that getting rid of mental clutter is an ongoing process, so be patient with yourself and make small changes that work for you.

When you follow these steps, you will reduce your mental clutter and be more able to have more time and make the changes you want in your life.

15. Physical clutter.

When your surroundings are full of clutter, you find your energy drains and you take longer to get things done. When you organise your working space, you can move forward and get other things completed quickly.

Physical clutter refers to an excessive number of items in a physical space, such as a room, office, or home. This clutter can include things like clothes, papers, books, and other objects that are scattered around and not properly organised or put away. Physical clutter can make a space feel chaotic, overwhelming, and crowded, and can also create obstacles to moving around or finding things easily. Dealing with physical clutter often involves decluttering and organising the space to create a more ordered and functional environment.

Physical clutter can have a significant impact on your mental well-being and overall quality of life. Here are some ways that physical clutter can affect you:

- Living or working in a cluttered environment can lead to increased stress and anxiety. The presence of clutter can make it more difficult to relax and focus, leading to feelings of overwhelm and unease.
- Clutter can be a major distraction and interfere with your ability to focus and complete tasks. It can also make it difficult to find important items, leading to a decrease in productivity.
- Research has shown that clutter can affect thought processes and decision-making abilities. A cluttered environment can overwhelm the brain and make it harder to make clear and informed decisions.
- Cluttered spaces can have a negative impact on your mood and overall sense of well-being. A cluttered environment can evoke feelings of frustration, guilt, and even shame.

- Clutter can create breeding grounds for dust and allergens, which can have a negative impact on your physical health. Cluttered spaces can also make it more difficult to clean and maintain good hygiene.
- Clutter can create tension and conflict in relationships, especially if individuals have different levels of tolerance for disorder. Disagreements over clutter and its management can strain relationships and cause additional stress.

Overall, physical clutter can have a profound impact on various aspects of your life, from your mental well-being to your relationships and overall productivity. Taking steps to declutter your space can help improve your quality of life and create a more peaceful and harmonious living environment

Here is how to do that:

- Begin by creating a plan of areas in your home that need decluttering. This will help you stay and focussed on the task at hand.
- Dedicate specific time blocks in your day to work on decluttering. This could be a few hours each day or a whole weekend dedicated to decluttering.
- Go through your belongings and sort them into categories such as keep, donate, sell, or throw away. Be ruthless in your decision-making and only keep items that you truly need or love.
- Invest in bins, baskets, and shelves, to help keep your belongings organised and easily accessible.
- Once you have decluttered your space, make it a habit to regularly declutter your belongings to prevent clutter from building up again.
- Consider donating or selling items that you no longer need or use. This can help reduce waste and benefit others who may find

value in your unwanted items.
- If decluttering feels overwhelming or if you have trouble letting go of certain items, consider seeking help from a professional or a friend or family member for support.

16. Make time for yourself.

It's easy to get caught up in the hustle and bustle of daily life, leaving little to no time for yourself. However, it is crucial to make time for yourself to maintain a healthy mind, body, and spirit.

Taking time out for yourself is not a luxury, but a necessity. It can be easy to neglect the most important relationship you have - the one with yourself. By planning to have moments in your busy schedule to focus on self-care and self-improvement, you can improve your overall well-being and quality of life.

Whether it's practising mindfulness, engaging in a hobby, setting aside time for exercise, or simply enjoying a moment of quiet reflection, making time for yourself is essential for recharging your mind and body.

If you've been feeling overwhelmed, stressed, or simply in need of a moment of peace and solitude, it's time to make time for self-care and discover the transformative power of taking care of yourself.

If you do things for other people most of your day, here are some tips to enable you to make time for yourself. This is important because it is vital to address your own needs for self-care that can only happen when you have the time to do this.

If you only look after others, not only do you not have the time for yourself but also there is a high possibility that your own health and welfare will suffer.

Plan what you want for yourself.

When you have a definite project in mind and you put it in your diary, then you are more likely to commit to it. Many people are rather vague about doing something 'when I have the time.'

Set realistic boundaries.

Decide how much time you will be engaged in doing things for others each day. Their demands may be endless and however obliging you are there will always be a point when you have to say 'no.' Make sure that when you stop there is enough time for yourself.

Engage with others affected by your plans. Unfortunately, if you are a caring and helping sort of person, other people expect you to always be available to carry out their needs. However, if you can explain how things will be different, why you cannot always be available to them, and how someone or something else will cover their needs, then you will be more able to use time for yourself.

Stick to your plans.

When you make a commitment to do more for yourself, be brave and don't waver from those plans (except with a dire emergency). Don't succumb to emotional blackmail but be assertive in keeping the time set aside for your own needs.

Increase the time for yourself.

Once you have started small and have time to do things you want to do, then be brave and increase the amount of personal time you have for yourself.

You find that the people you spend so much time doing things for will gradually accept the new you, as you find time for yourself. Not only that, but when you have the time for yourself, then when you work for other people, you do so with greater enthusiasm and energy.

When you are at home, you may use your time doing things for other members of your family or just keeping your home in order, but what about time for you?

It's vital to have sufficient time for yourself to address looking after your physical, emotional and spiritual needs in whatever way you find useful.

Here are some ways to increase the time you have for yourself.

Change your routines.

Decide to spend just half an hour doing something for yourself by stopping what you do for others earlier than usual.

17. Look after yourself.

Taking care of yourself is a fundamental aspect of maintaining overall well-being and living a fulfilling life. It can be easy to neglect your own needs and put those of others before those of yourself. However, by making self-care a priority, you can improve your physical, mental, and emotional health, leading to increased productivity, happiness, and resilience in the face of challenges.

Nurture and nourish your mind, body, and soul. By finding a deeper connection with yourself, you can develop a greater sense of self-awareness and inner peace, paving the way for a more balanced and harmonious life.

Having enough time to do all the things you would like to do is an ongoing challenge. When you analyse how much time you spend each day doing things others expect, you may think you have no choice but to continue in that way. However, you have choices and it's important to distinguish between what is in your job description and what you do for others because you think they expect you to do those things.

Sometimes you must stop doing things for other people so you can have more time for yourself. This is a delicate balance between what you do for you and what you do for others, especially what you perceive other people expect from you.

Everyone is used to having a particular role in life and in that role you believe that you 'should' behave in certain ways. Yet doing those things may use up so much of your time that you find it difficult to have enough time to do things which are important for you.

However, what you do for others may be things which are classified as 'shoulds.' Write the words: I should.... and fill in the blank as many times as you can. These are your 'shoulds' the things you feel other people expect from you.

Now, look at your list and change the 'I should' to 'if I choose to' and notice the difference in how you feel about it.

For example: 'I should telephone my parents every day.' to ' I telephone my parents every day, if I choose to.'

When you do this, you change the obligation to a choice. You may decide to carry out the same actions but do so willingly rather than with resentment. And you also give yourself the choice to not do so sometimes.

Louise Hay in her book 'You can Heal Your Life' talks about being 'self-ish.' This means putting your own needs first sometimes. This is vital to do if you want to have more time and a more balanced life.

Give yourself a choice. Others may encourage and support you to do more for yourself for your health and wellbeing. Unless you look after your own needs, you will be less efficient at dealing with other's needs and your own health and wellbeing will suffer.

18.Time management isn't easy.

The journey to mastering time management may not be easy, but with dedication and the right tools, it is achievable.

If you've been used to working long hours, always saying yes to whatever others ask of you and forgetting the importance of looking after yourself and your own self-care needs, then you may be challenged to manage your time more effectively.

Step by step you must learn to devise efficient ways to complete your tasks, so you aren't wasting time, to gain enough confidence not only to say 'no' to others but also 'no' to the task itself if no-one knows why it needs to be done at all.

Routines become habits that are rarely re-examined or re-assessed to check whether they still need to be done at all. How long is it since you thought rationally about your daily routine, and what you could stop doing altogether?

After you've decided what you can pass on to someone else and recognised and let go of time- wasters and been efficient for the rest, you can use the freed-up time to do something that you really enjoy. If you identify, in advance, what you will do with the newly created time, then you are much more likely to do it.

There are many ways to get yourself and your life more organised. If you are wasting time and opportunities regularly, then find and follow a way to use your day more efficiently and effectively.

Time management is a vital skill that plays a fundamental role in your daily life. From meeting deadlines at work to making time for friends and family, effective time management can lead to getting more done, reducing stress, and largely improved well-being. Take control of your time, boost your efficiency, and ultimately enhance your overall quality of life.

What can you do if you have a challenge with time management?

Delegate more: those tasks that someone else could do if you teach them what to do. It is easy to fall into the trap of believing that you are indispensable: you are not. However, don't expect the person you delegate to know exactly how to do it all straight away. Show them and then supervise them at first and give them helpful feedback. Once they know what to do and you are happy, then let them get on with it.

Stop doing things which no longer must be done. Often jobs become the norm, but circumstances change and when you step back and think you realise you can stop them.

Do things more efficiently. Streamline tasks. Get a colleague to give you feedback because the obvious is not so obvious when it's about you and the way you do things.

Are you ready to organise your time, your life and yourself to have a balanced life? Don't just read this, do something different, because if you continue with all the negative effects of poor time management, you will feel more and more stressed and overworked and frustrated.

If you are you ready to change, don't just read this book, do something different. If you continue with the negative effects of poor time management, you will feel more and more stressed and overworked and frustrated. Instead, do something different and change your life.

19. Ask for help.

Many people find themselves overwhelmed with the demands of their personal and professional lives, leading to feelings of stress and frustration.

Asking for help to manage time is not a sign of weakness, but rather a proactive step towards gaining control over your timetable and priorities.

Whether you're a busy professional juggling multiple projects or a student struggling to balance academics and extracurricular activities, learning how to ask for help in managing your time can be a game-changer. Reaching out for support can lead to increased productivity, reduced stress, and a greater sense of accomplishment.

When you find a task takes more of your day than you'd like it to and wonder if you'll ever get it done then remember it's OK to ask for some help because asking for help is a vital part of having more time for yourself.

Asking people do help is a simple thing to do but sometimes it can feel so daunting that you don't ask for what you need and struggle on, hoping that someone will read your mind and realise that you'd give anything for some help with the task in hand.

Yet for many people and maybe it is for you to, asking someone else to help is an incredibly difficult thing to do.

Maybe it's because there is no-one available to whom you could make a request for help, or maybe you don't like the idea of having to explain to someone exactly what to do, if they help you.

Your resistance may be because you believe, rightly or wrongly, that you must complete what you set out to do, without help. You may have deeply ingrained messages in relation to not giving up.

Yet there are tasks which you could easily ask for help from someone else. They are those tasks which you are doing now, but, although they have to be done, it's not vital they are done by you.

To delegate more effectively, you have to be clear about exactly what you want to other person to do, teach them how to do it, watch how they perform and then let them get on with it, but supervise them by having regular checks, especially initially, to find out if they are doing what you want them to do.

The result of getting help and delegating part of what you do routinely is free up more time each week.

The benefits of getting help mean you become less stressed, more relaxed, more able to think more clearly. You will not only free up a considerable amount of time, after the initial training you have to provide for the person helping you, but you will be more relaxed and more confident.

20. Making a difference.

Striking a balance between work, personal life, and self-care can be a daunting task, but with the right approach and mindset, it is possible to improve how you manage time and make a significant difference in your overall well-being.

Time management tips: try them to make a difference in your life.

⬦ When you get yourself organised the night before, you can sort out what you want to take to work the next day and have it prepared and ready for the morning.

⬦ If you have children to take to school before you arrive at work, make sure you get their things ready for school too, before you go to bed.

⬦ It's vital to have enough sleep. That may mean going to bed a bit earlier.

⬦ Set your alarm early enough to wake up and get yourself ready without panic or rush.

⬦ Always eat breakfast. For example, at least a bowl of cereal and some fruit will set you up well for the day. Skipping breakfast and surviving on coffee leads drop in blood sugar mid-morning and eating too much sugary food and to unhealthy eating later in the day.

⬦ If you drive to work, be sure before you have enough fuel because it will cause more stress to buy that on the way.

⬦ If you drive, devise a route to avoid lengthy hold ups. Going to work earlier may do this, anyway.

◈ Consider other ways to travel. If it's practical cycle and get your daily exercise without too much extra time taken in your day.

◈ If you travel by train or bus, you can use the time to think or catch up with reading, either journal reading or a novel.

◈ Arrive with a fresh mind and an exercised body ready to complete admin tasks before the extra work for the day begins.

21.Choose with whom you spend time.

When it comes to your social circle, the people you surround yourself with have a significant impact on your thoughts, behaviour, and overall well-being. Choosing who to spend your time with is a decision that should not be taken lightly, by making a conscious choice about who you let into your life, you create a more fulfilling and enriching environment that nurtures your best self.

When you think about changes you want to make to your life, including what and who irritates you, then you need to consider the people who are in your life and with whom you want to spend your time. You may find that there are some people who are always good company and you enjoy being with them. Others make your heart sink and you can't wait to get away from their company.

When you are at work, you may not have much choice about the people you have to spend your working hours with. It is worth taking the time to think about what it is about the people you don't like, the people who irritate you, and reflect on whether you also have the same traits yourself. For example, if you consider that someone is always unfriendly perhaps that is the way they think of you too. If that's the situation, you may find that your perception of them changes once you become more interested and friendly towards them.

If this person is someone who you have to work in the same office but find it difficult to concentrate while they chatter most of the time then take your courage in both hands and tell them you would prefer if they could not talk while you are trying to concentrate on the task in hand.

Perhaps they want to help you get something done, and you feel irritated because you think you can do it more quickly on your own. You have two choices here: either tell them without preamble: 'Sorry but I can do this on my own, I don't need any help from you,' or 'Let me explain more fully how to do this task and then I'll let you get on with it yourself.' For the latter choice you need to come to terms with delegating responsibility to the other person after you have explained the process to them.

If you go out socially with a group of people who you like that's great, but if you would rather do something else with others, then excuse yourself and follow your heart to do what you really want to do with the company of those you like. Life is too short to be with people you don't like. So decide and choose with whom you want to spend time with, whether this is at work or socially.

22. Successful people are experts.

Time management is a skill that sets successful people apart. The ability to efficiently allocate and prioritise tasks is essential in achieving goals and reaching greater milestones. From setting goals and deadlines to minimising distractions and delegating tasks, mastering time management is the cornerstone of success in any field.

Successful people use time efficiently, so they get tasks completed and achieve their goals.

Here are ways you can do this too:

Concentrate on what you are doing.

If you have something to do, focus on it with no distractions for a while. Notice the sort of things that distract you so that you can eliminate them. If people talking distract you, then work in a place where you can be on your own. If people constantly interrupt you or by telephone calls, then switch off your phone, close your door, let people know that at certain times you are not to be disturbed.

Make plans.

If you flit from one task to another so that things get forgotten as you find other things to grab your attention, then you must stop this habit by planning efficiently what you intend to do during a certain period. Making plans is about being specific about which part of your grand plan you will complete each day and then getting on and doing it before you do anything else.

Work efficiently.

If you have got into inefficient ways of working, then you must take a step back and assess what would be the most efficient way to do your tasks.

Sometimes another person can point out ways to save time by doing things in a more streamlined way. It's easy to become unaware of habits that could slow you down.

Talk to others.

When you talk to those involved in similar projects, it may surprise you to find they approach the work in different ways to the way you do. They may use more up-to-date technology, for example, or have their office arranged more effectively to cut down on time taken to do the work.

Know the small stuff.

Decide what someone else could do and then delegate. It's important to be aware of all the tasks involved in what you must do to achieve what you want. However, most successful people are very good at delegation, they are the experts who teach and advise others, and they do the jobs that only they can do.

Those things that either bore you because they are too easy or hinder you because you don't know how to do them quickly, you can delegate, so long as you keep an overview of the situation.

23. Steps to get things done.

It's easy to feel overwhelmed by the sheer number of tasks and responsibilities that constantly demand your attention. Whether it's professional projects, personal goals, or household chores, there always seems to be something waiting to be checked off your to-do list.

From setting clear objectives and selecting tasks to establishing a structured routine and using the right tools, each step plays a crucial role in maximizing your productivity. By fulfilling these plans into your daily life, you will not only harness your time and energy more efficiently but also experience a greater sense of accomplishment and satisfaction.

How often does this happen to you? You are trying to manage your time more effectively and you've decided what you want to get done. You've set aside a day to do it and then other things happen. The phone rings and that leads to having to look something up on the internet. While you are online, you decide to have just a quick look at your emails and there are some which need to have an urgent reply, or so you decide. Then the post arrives and you have to do some jobs after you've opened your letters. Just as you get down to the original task you realise you are feeling rather hungry so will have to make yourself something to eat or a friend is wondering if you might have lunch together.

So another day goes by and the task isn't complete.

Would you rather manage your day so that you get the jobs done, with no hassle and then could move on to other tasks and even have plenty of time of some rest and relaxation too? You could be like that if you follow the following 7 steps:

Set boundaries to stop distractions. Being interrupted and distractions are the two most important reasons you must be clear about boundaries. You set these but explain them to anyone who may want to cross them.

Do not answer the telephone, look at or answer emails, open letters, surf the internet or socialise while you get on with your task.

Be very specific. Decide what you are going o do in the time you set aside for the task. You may do part of a project which will take you many hours and days. However, define what you want to get done in the hour or the afternoon you decide to work on that project.

Stop when you have completed the job. Define the beginning and end of what you are doing today. Say to yourself, 'when I've done so and so I'll stop and take a break.' You can continue after that if you re-define what you plane to do and the time you are setting aside for it.

It's well known that people who make plans are more likely to achieve what they plan.

24. Finally.

Understanding time and how to manage it, can result in increased efficiency, reduced stress levels and an improved sense of accomplishment.

Once learned, time management can bring about positive changes, improving both quality of life overall as well as progress toward personal or professional development goals. If time management has become part of your life, then consider yourself among one of life's great achievers!

Time management involves more than simply planning out your day with a to-do list or having a routine schedule; it involves understanding how best to use your time for maximum productivity. A person skilled in managing their time understands that there's always a time and place for work, for relaxation, and for self-care.

Time management gives you the power to streamline daily activities, eliminate inefficiency, and decrease procrastination - leading to improved concentration levels and focus. This in turn decreases stress and anxiety levels significantly.

As soon as you've mastered time management, meeting deadlines and targets should no longer be an arduous challenge for you.

Your life can benefit immensely when you master time management. Allocating enough time between personal, social, and professional life is often difficult to balance; those who understand how to effectively allocate their time know the significance of maintaining a work-life balance - something which eventually leads to increased happiness and fulfillment in their life.

Time management also aids long-term career advancement. This requires both patience and constant learning, which may sometimes seem overwhelming with your workload. By developing effective time management skills, however, ample time for self-development activities becomes available allowing you to stay abreast of market trends, enhance skillsets and open doors to opportunities aligning with career objectives.

Health is another area that benefits significantly when time management skills are properly applied. People who master time effectively also make time for regular exercise, healthy meals and adequate sleep - as well as understanding its effect on productivity levels - which leads to a healthier lifestyle promoting both physical and mental well-being.

Time management is about more than simply getting things done; it's about taking charge of your life and being in control. Expert time management skills provide you with the ability to reduce stress, increase productivity, boost career development, and maintain a healthier work-life balance by efficiently using your precious time. Time management is an invaluable skill that will benefit every aspect of your life and should be considered an achievement worthy of praise. Though you may not know it immediately, your achievement represents an essential life skill which will propel you towards greater success in future endeavours.

Time management is an essential skill that can transform productivity and success across your life, both personal and professional. By learning time management skills, you gain control over your timetable, and you can select tasks effectively while allocating enough time for important activities and avoiding procrastination.

Effective time management gives you the power to meet deadlines, reduce stress and meet goals more efficiently. Setting clear goals, creating schedules and using tools such as calendars and to-do lists allows you to effectively manage your time and maximize productivity.

Mastering time management can not only boost your work performance, but it can also have a profound effect on your overall well-being. By allocating enough time for self-care, relaxation, and activities that bring joy, you can maintain a healthy work-life balance and avoid burnout.

Overall, time management is an invaluable skill that will enable you to achieve your full potential and live a more fulfilling and successful life. Congratulations on taking control through effective time management; there are endless possibilities when effectively managing time.

Ultimately, mastering time management not only leads to greater accomplishments and success but also allows you to have more time for leisure activities, self-care, and relationships. It is a skill that can be learned, and continuously improved upon, leading to a more balanced and fulfilling life.

Don't miss out!

Visit the website below and you can sign up to receive emails whenever Susan Kersley publishes a new book. There's no charge and no obligation.

https://books2read.com/r/B-A-EFNC-HQRQ

BOOKS 2 READ

Connecting independent readers to independent writers.

Did you love *More Time for You Now*? Then you should read *How to Have a Balanced Life*[1] by Susan Kersley!

[2]

Chaotic life? Never get much done? Want more balance?

Simple changes can give you big results.

Are you neglecting important aspects of your life because you don't have enough balance? Do you struggle to achieve what you want?

Let Susan Kersley guide you through simple steps to reach your goals, find more balance and rediscover forgotten parts of yourself.

The author is a retired medical doctor and was a life coach for fifteen years.

How to have a balanced life is a well written, concise personal development book with easy to follow suggestions that will make a big

---

1. https://books2read.com/u/brlLzm

2. https://books2read.com/u/brlLzm

Also by Susan Kersley

A Novel
Pills and Pillboxes
Connection Deception

Books about Weight Management
Change Your Mind, Change Your Weight
Weight Loss Success
Mind Over Weight

Books for Doctors
ABC of Change for Doctors
Life After Medicine
Prescription for Change
Lifestyle Coaching for Doctors
The Busy Doctor's Guide: Improve your Work-Life Balance
Work-Life Balance for Doctors
Simple Ways to Meet the Challenges of Working as a Doctor
Meet the Challenges of Working as a Doctor

Retirement Books
Get Ready for Retirement
Life After Work
Retirement: Back to Basics

Self-help Books
How to Have a Balanced Life
69 Easy Ways to Change Your life
15 Ways to Change Your Life
Connect and Change
Coping With New Year Resolutions
How to Change Your Life
Improve Your Work Life Balance
More Time for You Now

Watch for more at https://susankersley.co.uk.

About the Author

Susan Kersley has written personal development and self-help books for doctors and others, and books about retirement and novels.

She was a doctor for thirty years and then left Medicine to be a Life Coach..

Now retired, she is updating her books and writing more. Please visit her website https://susankersley.co.uk

If you enjoyed this book, **please take a moment to leave a review.** Reviews are so important for independent authors.

Read more at https://susankersley.co.uk.